CW00340326

Of Death and a Banana Skin

OF DEATH AN

BANANA

SKIN

Simon Mayor

Acoustics

Of Death and a Banana Skin
Simon Mayor

ISBN: 978-0-9522776-7-5

First edition 2018

First published in 2018 by
Acoustics Publishing
PO Box 350
Reading RG6 7DQ
England
acousticspublishing.com

Typographical consultant Ian Dennis
Illustrations © Hilary James 2018
Edited by Hilary James
Photograph on page 34 courtesy of Berkshire Record Office

contents

augmented reality

Many of the pages in this book can be brought to life by
scanning them with a tablet computer or smartphone.
This will access animations, readings, music and other media.

For instructions please visit simonmayor.com/banana-skin

CD and download

An accompanying album is available of readings, songs
and instrumental music by Simon Mayor & Hilary James.

Please visit simonmayor.com/banana-skin

WE

Hilary James first persuaded me to read a poem during a concert. It was The Stick, and people seemed to like it.

For years we had performed together on stage, she singing (mostly), me playing (mostly), but we both did both. This was usually as a duo, but also with our mandolin quartet The Mandolinquents and in other occasional configurations.

Perhaps I'll be more specific about my poems and her means of persuasion. She got me in an armlock, twisted it violently up my back before threatening to push it that extra inch to tear the tendons, thus preventing me from playing the mandolin ever again. SAS training is so rigorous it becomes instinctive.

The thought of not playing the mandolin was unthinkable, but after thinking about it, I thought it best to succumb, and just a few years later this book seems to be happening.

Secretly, I'm convinced it was all because she wanted to do the illustrations.

simonmayor.com

A YORK-SHIRE-MAN IN THE SOUTH

I used to live next door to Reading Reading Centre. You might want to read that sentence again out loud if you dare and ponder the depths of absurdity to which presumably educated human beings can sink. OK, politicians have been guilty of worse, but really, of all the inexplicably confusing names you could bestow upon an institution, Reading Reading Centre surely takes the biscuit (and up to 1976 that very biscuit could have been supplied by Huntley & Palmer's factory just half a mile away). They could have called it Reading Literacy Centre, for goodness sake! At least the uninitiated local and many a fazed foreigner would have had a sporting chance of pronouncing it correctly. Even Books 'R' Us or Phonics-U-Like might have been preferable. It wouldn't have been so bad had 'Reading' the town, kept to its original 'Redding', but no, the English language has always taken smug delight in its proclivity for confusion.

Reading is ridding itself of a bad press, slowly but surely. Even Her Maj thought fit to get the bus down from Windsor to open the new railway station for us. Since student days (a degree in Russian Studies doomed by a preference for playing the mandolin) the town has been home, and, despite a few moves, I've clung to the same square mile like a cat to its territory ever since. It lends a sense of stability to life as a touring musician. In that time, 45 years and counting, 'home' has transformed itself from a two-storey red-brick backwater into a vibrant, sleepless mini-metropolis, as cosmopolitan as London, European base for many international companies, and proud home of The Oracle Centre, a vast retail cathedral built at the turn of the millennium. Reading can now impressively and justifiably claim to be the place where people from Slough go shopping. What an honour to live here!

But the Yorkshireman never really left me either. In the early days there were times when both the locals and my new southerner friends at university would greet with blank incomprehension my flat vowels and completely innocent use of dialect. One quickly learns to speak standard English, doesn't one? The accent remains, though, albeit softened a little by the years.

Nowadays, regular trips to The Yorkshire Dales to indulge in some hillwalking keep me in touch with my roots and lend opportunity for nostalgic excursions into the vernacular. One summer, a friend and I took the train to Richmond and walked west for a few days, stopping at cheap guest houses until we reached The Lake District. About a mile before the Lancashire border we were engaged in lengthy conversation by an old Tyke out cutting his hedge. After half an hour the world was definitely a better place and Yorkshire cricket had been analysed in some depth. We were taking our leave when he asked if I was a Yorkshireman.
'Yes, Sheffield', I replied.
'Only just', he grudgingly conceded. 'What about you?' He turned to my friend.
'Leicestershire' came the reply.
'That'll do.' He looked away. 'Thought you might be one of these bloody Lancastrians.'

Studying Russian, which began at school in Sheffield, had been a revelation. Getting to grips with the alphabet was the easy bit, and how wonderful that, once over this initial hurdle, the spelling was so logical. A major simplifying revision in 1917 meant that to see a word in print was to be confident of its pronunciation. My accent was always good too; the musical ear helped. Later, at university, the native speaker who took us for conversation classes complimented me one day.

'Simon, your accent is so good that when I close my eyes and listen to you, you could almost be Russian. You have only two problems: grammar and vocabulary.'

I knew the Cyrillic script was on the wall so far as any career in academia was concerned, but in any case, a passion for the forgotten beauty of the mandolin had long since overtaken any such aspirations.

As a musician one inevitably becomes acutely aware of pulse, of rhythm. Working with a singer (Hilary James who also illustrates this book) awakens a deep admiration for those who write well-crafted, wittily rhymed song lyrics, and indeed writing songs oneself underlines how hard this can be. There's an uncharitable quip that a poet is just a songwriter who can't write a tune. In truth, the two are different art forms in the same medium, words. But it's also true that even without melody, rhyme and rhythm draw in the listener, engage the ear, and for me, remain the zestiest condiment to the written or spoken word.

From a personal perspective, professional life has centred around the mandolin, mostly performing and recording, but also writing tuition and repertoire books, music journalism, and, in recent years, hosting weekend Mandolin Retreats. The first few of these, gratifyingly well attended, were in the south of England and it was decided to promote one in the neglected North, with a comfortable hotel in home town Sheffield as venue.

To my delight, bookings came in from far and wide, including one from an American who was as keen to see Yorkshire as he was to play the mandolin. His wife was accompanying him on the extended trip, and he wrote how they both adored films set in the county: Calendar Girls, A Private Function, The Full Monty... it was a long list. The problem was, they always watched with subtitles because they found the Yorkshire accent impenetrable, so he was hoping I didn't have one when I taught mandolin...? I emailed back with the bad news, but all seemed well when we met and I hope he left as a better mandolin player.

Ilkley is now the usual base on trips north, a town with a Roman, and before that, a Celtic history. It is beautiful in a somewhat austere, Pennine way, with some true architectural gems hidden among the already imposing Victorian gritstone grandeur. Seek out Heathcote, a mansion by Lutyens or The White House, a private dwelling which is a particularly fine example of Bauhaus design. I first made Ilkley's acquaintance because musician friends there offered a 'safe house' on any sojourn north. Over many visits I enjoyed not only the charms of the surrounding countryside, but the convenience of being just a short train journey from both Leeds and Bradford, and all the cultural benefits of that broad conurbation. Pierce Ilkley's own genteel veneer ('morning coffee at Betty's?'), and you'll soon discover its own cultural life to be the envy of many a small place, Ilkley Literature Festival being one of the largest in the country. Ilkley Moor, setting for the title poem of this collection, is an inescapable, brooding, dominating presence, towering over the town from the south and fond of blocking any late afternoon sun. But Ilkley wouldn't be Ilkley without its famous Moor, and the associated Yorkshire national anthem On Ilkley Moor Bar T'at (translation: On Ilkley Moor Without A Hat). Best not tell a Yorkshireman its tune is from Kent.

In 2001 the outbreak of foot and mouth disease struck the nation, and, like other areas of open country, Ilkley Moor was closed to hikers lest infection be spread by boots. We all miserably but dutifully complied with the ruling; the problem was, nobody told the sheep, who blithely wandered down into the town for company and to eat the grass by the main street, The Grove. Photographs of them listening to the municipal Saturday afternoon entertainment on the green in front of the bandstand remain among my most treasured.

The Grove closes completely on certain days to host larger scale attractions. Nifty Fifties night comes around every year, attracting jive dancers from as far away as Leeds. The touring French market turned out to be the one place not to address the beret-bedecked olive seller in French ('dunno wot yer on abaht pal, I'm from Bingley'); but best of all is Ilkley's own improvement on The Royal Albert Hall's Last Night Of The Proms. The Grove is a sea of Prosecco and fluttering Union Jacks while a couple of opera singers give their all.
'In London y'af to mek doo wi' a bloody symphony orchestra; 'ere y'gerra proper silver band an' y'can 'ave a tipple or two wi'aht werritin' abaht drivin' 'om!'

While music rears its head (how could it not?) as do other subjects including echoes of many years writing for both adults and children, the towns and environs of Reading and Ilkley have provided inspiration for much of this volume. Refreshingly and reassuringly they shatter the stereotypical descriptions of the supposed North-South divide.

Unfriendly, decadent southerners who have to drink rubbish beer? Not in Reading! Dark, satanic mills and people 'toiling on'? Not in Ilkley! In their own ways they're both inspiring and uplifting places that mirror, I hope, my own optimism and in turn the spirit of the poems here.

By Middlesmoor I found a staff, a sturdy stick
That, shed from barren beeches, bid me bend to pick
It from the land,
To help me stand,
And more, to walk the walk I'd planned
And finish, though with aching thighs, with smiles
Novembery Nidderdale's inspiring miles.

So stout with staff, I found a pace, a quicker pace
Cross slippery rocks. But watery whispers asked: 'Why race
Me to the sea?
For you are free
To linger or just to stop and be.
I have a flow, and with it I must go.
Just go with yours, my dale to better know.'

And as I slowed, so slowed the dale, the Nidd, the scudding sky.
And only then saw I the heron, hare and heard the cry
From distant rocks
Of Mr Fox.
And even though he stalks
Some hapless prey, he still has time to meet my gaze
Across a dripping field on this, his hungriest of days.

STICK

And only then I saw the timid trout, who, caressed
By currents, like a breeze-blown hawk held motionless
Against the flow.
If I should throw
A playful pebble, then I know
He'll dart into the shallow safety of the reeds.
Yes, I have slowed, but how my heart now speeds.

And as the tearoom talk of Pateley Bridge drew near,
I thought to cast the stick; just let it go with conscience clear.
But wait! Don't throw!
Best lay it by the lane, and so
It may another weary walker lure
To march it back to Middlesmoor.

An actual experience, with just a dash of poetic licence. It was composed on the move and then hurriedly scribbled on a paper bag in the tearoom in Pateley Bridge. The third and fourth stanzas were added a few days later.

BANANA
ON ILKLEY MOOR

Wi' an angry wind so blows today,
And who would challenge what most say,
That only mad men choose to stray
Beyond the shelter these four walls
    Afford from winter's squalls?

Mad? Maybe, but nonetheless,
In coat and hefty boots I'll dress,
And up to t'top o' t'moor I'll press.
My eccentricities forgive –
    It's just the way I live.

Shall I tek a drink or owt to munch?
Nah! I'll get back down in time for lunch.
Just one banana – t'best o' t'bunch.
I'll tek it wi' me just in case
    I need to stuff me face.

So off I climbed, and half way up
From peaty pools well chilled I supped,
And quenched me thirst from both hands cupped.
Mouth and gullet lubricating,
    Stamina rejuvenating...

17

... Or so I thought, but this was humbling -
T'moor had got me panting, stumbling,
And then I thought, 'me tummy's rumbling!'
And so I pulled out of me pack
      Me yellow, fruity snack.

I found a stone, well sheltered, flat,
And buckling down me 'Biggles' hat,
I contemplated life and that,
Before I peeled the leathery skin,
      And sunk me gnashers in.

Its fruity sugars circulating
Round me veins were soon placating
Hunger pains from irritating
Gastric juices. Who could quibble
      Stopping for a nibble?

'Well thanks!' Me stomach juices cried,
For hunger had been satisfied!
This moor I'll tek now in me stride.
But now I've had me little meal,
      What to do wi' t'peel?

See – I'm a rambler, old-school, proud.
I'll walk neath sun, neath threatening cloud,
I'll walk wherever I'm allowed,
And other places I'll admit,
      Though none would know of it.

For I leave no trail, no human clue.
I'll tread on stones to foil those who
Might trace me tracks. And if me shoe
Would fall in mud, what print remains
     Is washed by t'next day's rains.

So, back to my banana skin!
I walked well wide of where I'd been
And found a rocky cleft wherein
I let it lay. No-one would know
     The stone it hid below.

Then I slung me pack, pulled up me socks,
And off I shot to t'top o' t'rocks
Like Usain Bolt off t'startin' blocks.
I parked me bum right down on t'ground
     And gaped at t'spectacle around.

North, south, east… how I was blessed
With such fine scenery, Yorkshire's best.
And then I turned and looked to t'west.
Bloody Lancashire! That's all I need!
     So I turned and gazed at Leeds.

I found a pen inside me coat,
Some paper too, and then I wrote
In rhyming verse this anecdote,
At least the tale I've so far told,
     But t'denouement will unfold…

Summer, Autumn, Winter faded,
Two years passed, and oft in jaded
Mood I pondered how degraded
Might now be that jaundiced rind
     Wherein I once had dined.

Now, three years on, sometimes, unsure
Of what I'll find, this strange allure
Compels me climb up Ilkley Moor
To find the secret rocky cleft
     And gaze on what I left.

Racked by rain and feral frost,
Sad remains of life now lost,
Unlikely tropical compost.
Wizened, twisted, shrunken, black,
     There go we all, no turning back.

And so, to play life's pantomime.
I'll leave me 'at at 'ome and climb
Them peaty slopes for t'final time.
But comfort to me soul you'd bring
     If I might hear you sing:

'Wheer 'as tha bin since I saw thee?'

I went bar t'at on Ilkley Moor;
I caught me death o' cowd for sure,
Fell in t'peat and sunk right in,
     Just like a ruddy 'nana skin.

BELLS

Bluebells bloom in Middleton Woods
Quite late each year, the old Tyke tells,
At least compared to Berkshire's bells
(If they survive the wind, the floods).
So Southerner, take this advice:
When bluebells bend in Berkshire journey
North, that you might take
Communion with bluebells twice.

Brass bells clang on Ilkley Moor
Each morn at who-knows-when-and-why?
They tell me not the hour, but try
To drag me to St Margaret's door
By peeling out my godless guilt
For all of Ilkley, Middleton to hear.
But louder, louder they accuse,
So deeper sink I neath my quilt.

In Middleton Woods the bluebells ring,
Deafening only to the eyes
Of old Tykes who, from quilts would rise
– (Eventually!) and with them sing
A hymn of gentle, blue-green beauty.
While brass may stir me from my sleep,
The woodland bids me guiltlessly to rise
And walk for pleasure, not for duty.

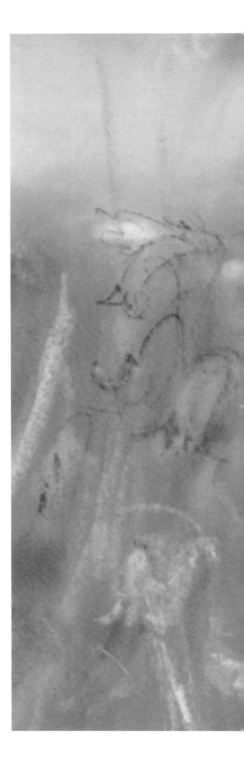

THE RAMBLER

At random speeds, at random heights,
Puffed up in random greys and whites,
The clouds from Lancashire skim low
And wait for wind on Beamsley Beacon,
Swallowing the summit, where a resting rambler (who,
With no beguiling view),
Now stands and hoists his pack
So he can
Back
To Addingham. As well he might!

Within these walls, I sit here dry
I sit here warm, and wait to spy
The rambler step below the mist.
He's there! Sure-footed, tumbling down
The rocks he bounces with a cautious haste (well-practised lest
Hard rain his Gortex test).
Though I can't see, I'd swear
No frown
He'll wear
Upon his face, for home is nigh.

Whatever clouds may eastwards flee
From blue-green Lancashire, you'll see
Me step beyond the tea-stained Wharfe
And on into the hills. Be damned
Hard rain, you feeble foe! In cast-off tweeds, in boots near-wrecked,
And hairy head bedecked
In wide-brimmed, oily hat,
The rambler
That
You spy tomorrow will be me.

Low Mill nestles,
Scrubbed and sandy wall to wall,
Where garden centre statuettes
Guard four-wheel drives parked up on burnished setts,
And windows with a rippled sheen
Cling close to doors in Cooking Apple Green
(A shade by Farrow & Ball).

Low Mill nestles,
Cradled in the river's crook,
One road out and one road in,
Comfy in its cul-de-saccy skin.
'Addingham? You're best to walk.
But take my word, from how the lads all talk,
There's nowt – but take a look.'

Low Mill nestles,
Cosy as the feather bed
From which you rose one misted morn
And stared me through as though since I was born
I'd worn these clothes and trudged this lane
To weave the cloth, a meagre wage to gain.
'Ow do?' I softly said.

Low Mill wrestles,
With its then and now, a strain
To play its game of make believe. As
Flat-capped ghosts of toiling textile weavers
Greet you well, you sense our chill.
But now, one short commute, three miles until
You take the Ilkley train.

LOW MILL

Riot at Low Mill, 1826

The now residentially desirable nook of Low Mill hides from the A65, tucked away at the end of a mile long cul-de-sac by a bend in the River Wharfe. From the last of the old weavers' cottages, a footpath takes over from the lane to offer a pleasant stroll upstream to Addingham.

The mill itself was constructed in 1788 by John Cunliffe, and is credited as being the first successful worsted mill in the world. The workers' cottages were built shortly afterwards. All went well until 1826 when the introduction of machinery to replace the hand loom weavers triggered riots; men intent on destroying the new technology converged from as far afield as Lancashire. An ex gratia offer of money for food was seen as no permanent solution, and, with starvation looming, a riot broke out. The building was initially defended by the management and some local workers, who eventually resorted to firearms. The next day, the then owner Jeremiah Horsfall requested, and was granted, military assistance in the form of a troop of Dragoon Guards. A stand-off ensued, with the protestors eventually marching further up the valley to attack mills in Skipton and Gargrave. Many arrests were made, with some men even being sentenced to death.

The riot at Low Mill has been cited as the first significant example of self-defence by organised labour, an episode that spawned the wider workers' movement and eventually the birth of the Labour Party.

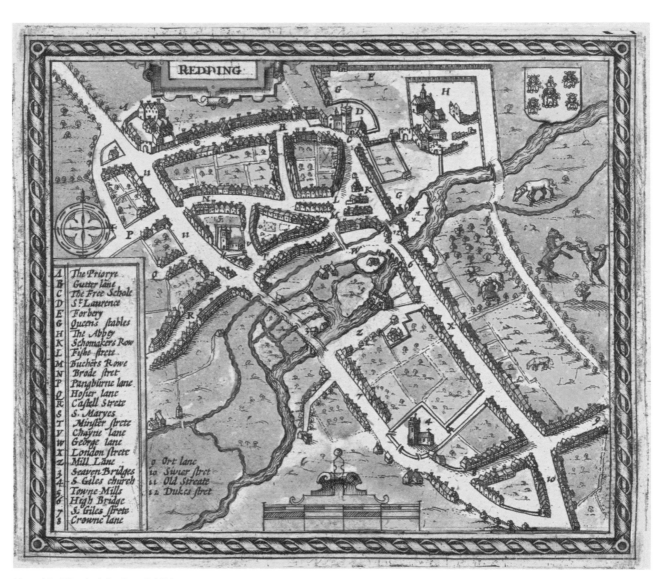

Map of Redding by John Speed, 1611

FROM READING

Canada was the destination for our very first trip across the Atlantic, and in retrospect I was rather pleased this was the case. Canada is like the korma a curry virgin eats before moving onto the phal that is the United States. It causes but the mildest of sweats, easily assuaged by a rather splendid supersize ice cream. We would regularly be asked where in England we lived. Not thinking for a moment that anyone would have heard of Reading, we'd simply reply 'near London'. The concept of 'near', I later discovered, means different things to different peoples. Two hundred and eighteen miles apart, Ilkley and Reading would never be described as

'near' by an English person, but a Russian I once met who professed to be from 'near' Moscow, turned out to live five hundred miles distant.

One Canadian pressed us for more information.
'You won't have heard of it, but we live in Reading. It's 40 miles west of London.'
'You live in Reading? You actually live in Reading?!?'

Unbeknown to us, our adopted town had unwittingly achieved celebrity status in Canada through a long running CBC radio programme called As It Happens. Started in 1968, the show mixes current affairs and general magazine content, and from its outset has always expressed the

location of anywhere as being so many miles from Reading, a surreal idiosyncrasy passed from presenter to presenter down the years. It's a gentle humour, typical of Canadians as we discovered over many subsequent visits. One programme host, Barbara Budd, reportedly described Reading as 'obscure', but added 'It will always have a very special place in my heart'. I can feel a little tear welling as I type, but sadly cannot report ever being aware of hordes of Canadian tourists invading the town every summer.

Nowadays, when in Canada and asked of our domicile, we always answer 'zero miles from Reading'.

27

Four Reading Sonnets

The Oracle

The Oracle shopping centre was constructed in 1999, opening in time for the millennium celebrations, and at a time when Western capitalism – and consumerism – marched headily onwards after the fall of the Eastern Bloc. It spans the river Kennet and occupies land once owned by Simonds brewery. Reading is traditionally known for its three Bs: biscuits, bulbs and beer, although all three industries have now vacated the town.

Queen Victoria Street

In a town, like so many, ravaged by post-war architecture, Queen Victoria Street – or at least its upper storeys – remains one of Reading's most attractive reminders of its unconcreted, red-brick past.

Reading Gaol

Most famous for holding Oscar Wilde for the now incomprehensible 'crime' of homosexuality, Reading Gaol closed in 2016 and for a brief period opened to the public. At the time of writing its future is uncertain.

Reading Abbey

Henry I founded Reading Abbey in 1121 and it continued to operate as a religious centre until Henry VIII's Dissolution of the Monasteries in 1538. It has since been in an increasingly sorry state of repair but now reopening after extensive renovation. Holy Brook, a partial diversion of the river Kennet, was excavated by the monks to drive mill wheels and feed fish ponds.

THE ORACLE

For centuries the leaden Kennet flowed
And wild wood bison grazed. How long? Who knows?
But then the towering Oracle arose
Upon the banks that once were buffaloed.

We blinked! And then our red-brick town was here:
The biscuits, bulbs, the Simonds IPA.
Now this! A caustic retail bliss. Some say
The town smelled sweeter when it still brewed beer.

And from the west-coast cafés we survey
This la-la land of architectural wit,
These pointless stairs that go nowhere. Admit:
We are seduced. We shop as blue chip prey.

And from its bendy bridge the two of us
Gaze down. The Kennet flows, oblivious.

QUEEN VICTORIA STREET

The creamy cheeks and terracotta bones
Of stoney Queen Victoria, bricks cast
Within this town, still smiling, colourfast,
Look down upon the street she calls her own.

And though her feet in concrete shoes are shod,
More hidden than her tables under paint,
Than boarded doors, one day we'll reacquaint
Ourselves with cobblestones that once were trod.

Above, slate grey, her hair is gripped in place
Within stout nets that serve as well to best
Arrest invading pigeons, gulls who'd nest
Among the nooks and crannies of her face.

And, unaware of regal smiles, the drone
Of Reading drowns the ringtone of my phone.

READING GAOL

With buttressed thumbs in red-brick braces broad,
The haughty walls of Reading Gaol incline
With high judicial arrogance, a sign
That timely fate awaited those outlawed.

With vain Victorian pomp arose its tower,
And eyed with sour disdain those who might pace
The Forbury, The Kennetside. Beware this place!
This monument to governmental power.

For near two dogged centuries the regime
Ruled. And inmates, hooded, hungry, chained,
Would cherish hope – what ghastly scraps remained.
Might they from lonely cells their souls redeem?

Today, past photographs of those it kept,
We queue to see the room where Oscar slept.

READING ABBEY

So shy, it hides what flinty walls remain
In corners known to few but those who may
Here dwell. But seek, and hold its stones, its clay,
And breathe once more the air of Henry's reign.

Six miles of eager, pious toil it took
To cut from Arrowhead to Abbey Mill,
Baptising fishponds, grinding wheels until
It found the Kennet. This was Holy Brook.

Old portly Henry did his bit – oh yes!
As though the weathering years were not enough,
He took his chance by calling Roman bluff,
And played, and won at high-stakes godly chess.

While Holy Brook beneath a tarmac floor
Still flows. The Abbey walls echo no more.

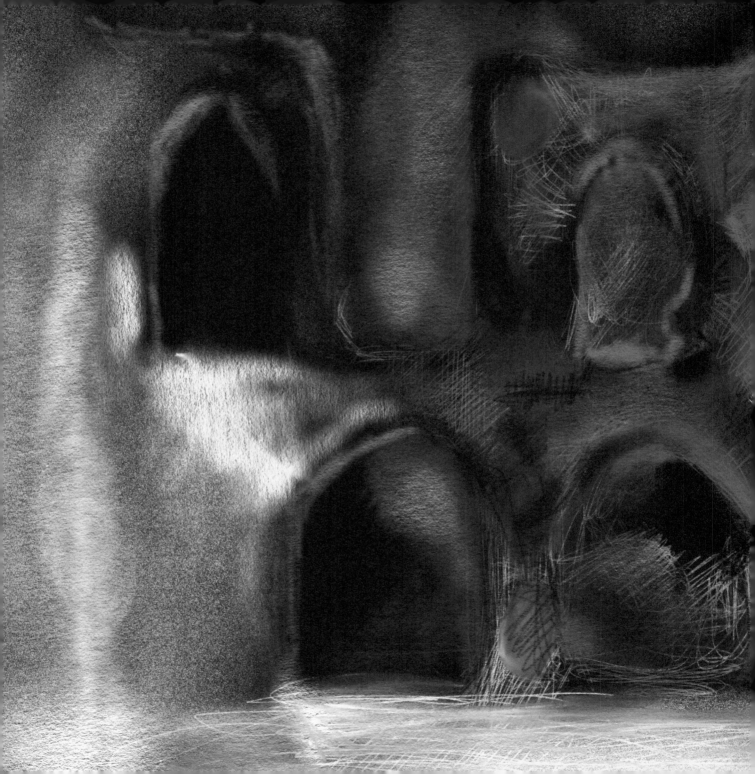

SUMER IS ICUMEN IN

It would be a criminal omission not to mention what is arguably Reading's greatest glory.

Born of a vibrant Thames Valley artistic life and considered to be of even greater cultural longevity than The Oracle Centre or even The Inner Distribution Road, Sumer Is Icumen In is a simple but inspiring ditty in the form of a round. It was discovered in Reading Abbey, and is thought to be the earliest known example of written music, dating from the mid 13th century. The song has cropped up regularly in more modern times, notably in the opening ceremony of the 1972 Munich Olympics and the horrifying closing scene of the 1973 film The Wicker Man.

The age of the manuscript alone would attract attention, but intriguingly, the scribe offers a choice of secular lyrics in Middle English or a religious text in Latin. The former has been widely translated into modern English, and, amid much pastoral rejoicing at the arrival of summer, contains what is thought to be the first written reference to farting, in this case by bucks ('bucke uerteþ'), joining in with the lowing cattle and bleating ewes, an enthralling orchestration.

The text, a modern translation, and some additional stanzas are offered overleaf with no fear of ribaldry.

Svmer is icumen in, lhude sing cuccu.
Groweþ sed and bloweþ med,
And springþ þe wde nu,
Sing cuccu.

Awe bleteþ after lomb lhouþ after calue cu;
Bulluc sterteþ, bucke uerteþ.

Murie sing cuccu, cuccu, cuccu,
Wel singes þu cuccu,
Ne swik þu nauer nu.

Sing cuccu nu, sing cuccu.
Sing cuccu, sing cuccu nu.

   (Anon)

Summer has come in, loudly sing cuckoo.
The seed grows and the meadow blooms,
And the wood springs anew,
Sing cuckoo.

Ewe bleats after lamb, cow lows after calf;
Bullock stirs, buck farts.

Merrily sing cuckoo, cuckoo, cuckoo,
Well you sing cuckoo,
Never stop now.

Sing cuckoo now, sing cuckoo.
Sing cuckoo, sing cuckoo now.

   (modern translation)

AUTUMN IS ICUMEN IN

Autumn is icumen in,
The cucu's buggered off!
Torrential rains
Have filled the drains,
And leaves have blocked the gutter troughs.
Prepare for colds and coughs!

Winter is icumen in,
The cucu's safe abroad.
And who could blame?
I'd do the same
Until the crippling snows had thawed,
If wings I might afford.

Springtime is icumen in,
The cucu's back from flight,
Upon a quest
To wrest a nest
From warblers, heedless to the blight
Of this sly parasite.

Sumer is icumen in,
So with the cucu sing
An ancient round
On ancient ground,
And make the Abbey Ruins ring -
A new awakening.

Swans nest, swans flock
From Kennet Mouth to Sonning Lock.
The food of Kings, I'd heard:
Regal, distant, unperturbed,
As white as any wedding frock.

Scan their lines. You will see
How we two glide expectantly,
Ranked as equals, yet apart,
A spike in nature's colour chart,
As black as ever swans could be.

Gulls, pigeons overhead,
Through gargling geese with wings a-spread
We break a passage, pulling rank,
And watchful, wait beside the bank
Wait for children. Wait for bread.

WANS

Children gather, children stand.
Stale crusts fly from sticky hands,
And some we catch in passing flight
And trigger squeals of raw delight.
The morning goes as planned!

Crumbs shaken, families gone,
The bridal party moves along.
But curious, vocal, prepossessed
With those who'd by the river rest,
The black swans linger long.

RED KITE

red kite
high flight
keen sight
just might
spy food
he knows
keep those
eyes glued

why kill?
hang still
wait 'til
wolf will
no theft
to eat
what meat
he's left

on wing
rising
his thing
gliding
winds blow
him where
he'll care
to go

The UK Wolf Conservation Trust at Beenham, just outside Reading, is open to the public on certain days. Feeding time attracts not only enthralled children (and mature poets), but large numbers of red kites with eyes on the leftovers.

45

BACK TO SCHOOL

In the late 1970s and early 1980s Hilary James and I played in countless folk clubs. The scene was particularly vibrant in those days and a tour of one small area, say, the North East of England, taking in a 30 mile radius of Newcastle, could take a couple of weeks. Our abiding memory is of warm, intimate gigs which we invariably played through a fog of Capstan Full Strength rising from the front row just a couple of feet in front of us. We had to take the decision to stop playing in smoke; the toll on Hilary's voice was simply too much, and even in those bad old days we were aware of the dangers of secondary smoking. While theatres and arts centres were always smoke free, it was nigh impossible to introduce a no smoking clause into our contracts for clubs. So for entirely philanthropic reasons, which had the pleasantly surprising side effect of rebalancing our finances, we decided to develop a show for children which was both educational and fun, and began to tour primary schools (shortly to be rebranded by the government as Universities of the First Age).

I soon discovered that children behave in an entirely different way from adults. If adults are not enjoying the show, they still clap politely (thank you!), but children fidget, stare round the room and eventually turn their back on you and start chatting to a neighbour. It was baptism by fire. I quickly learned never to ask an audience of children a direct question (try it - it's no fun), and discovered tricks of juvenile crowd control known to generations of teachers. The shows went well, and were immensely satisfying, but completely devoid of the ego massage on offer from an enthusiastic audience of grown-ups.

There were a couple of times, though, when I thought things might be different.

arrying the instruments
cross the playground after
ne concert, I was mobbed by
wo hundred infant school
hildren needing to dissipate
ome surplus energy.

t first it seemed amusing,
aguely flattering, like a
atered down version of The
eatles at Shea Stadium, but
his wolf pack was out of
ontrol and smelled blood.
efore I knew it, they'd
ecided they wanted souvenirs
nd, as my clothes were being
ulled this way and that, and
 desperately tried to hold on
o the guitar and mandolin, I
ecame truly frightened.
ilary to the rescue! Fists on
ips, and feet firmly spread
ike Brown Owl about to give

instructions on how to
decorate plant pots, she
summoned her finest
schoolmistressy tones,
clapped her hands vigorously,
and then with a wagging
finger told them to leave her
little boy alone!

It worked perfectly, but my
crumpled clothes, and,
metaphorically, my ego, were
now splattered with sticky,
sugary patches and chocolate
stains. I was left trembling.

Lone wolves can be no less
intimidating. In a career
that began in 1976 I have been
asked for my autograph on
maybe half a dozen occasions,
such are the dizzying heights
of celebrity reached by

mandolinists. After a show at
a primary school in the
1980s, a shy little girl came
up, and with eyes fixed on her
shoes muttered 'autograph'. I
was thrilled; this had never
happened to me before. I asked
if she had an autograph book
but she shook her head. I
fumbled around in my pockets
and eventually found a pen
and a piece of paper, but as I
was about to write my name she
took the pen from me and wrote
'Christine'. This time
looking me straight in the
eye, she proudly gave me the
piece of paper back. I could
do no more than offer my
profuse thanks.

KING CANUTE A

Now King Canute of England had a palace up in Oldham,
With lots of grovelling servants who did everything he told 'em.

He bellowed out his orders and he made his fingers click,
And anything he wanted would appear in half a tick.

But kings get bored in palaces, so soon he did decide
He'd like to spend a day just messing about at the seaside.

He said 'I'll go to Cleethorpes! Get my bucket, get my spade.'
And there upon the beach a royal sandcastle was made.

All day he built his battlements beside the salty seas,
And then he had his supper – fish and chips and mushy peas.

His snivelling servants said, 'Oh King! Your sandcastle is wondrous,
But is it strong enough to stand against these waves that break so thunderous?'

'I shall turn the tide' he said, 'I'll summon up my power.'
They said: 'Well get a move on 'cause it's due in half an hour.'

He cried: 'This castle I have made from Cleethorpes' soggy sand
Shall never ever be destroyed, forever it will stand.

Go back! Go back! You wayward waves, for I, the King, command it!'
But waves do not speak English, and they didn't understand it.

LEETHORPES

Up the sand the breakers crashed. Oh, it was a dreadful sight
To see him start to shiver and his tootsies turn all white.

'Go back! Go back!' He screamed and screamed until his face was blue,
'For I am King Canute and much more powerful than you!'

But ever inwards came the waves, and frankly it was shocking
To see the way his horribly knobbly kneecaps started knocking.

The water rose above his waist but still he cried 'Go back!
If I'd intended getting wet I would have brought my mac.'

By now the royal sandcastle was getting slightly wet.
'You wild and wicked waves' he seethed, 'I'll make you turn back yet.'

But the sea refused to listen and soon covered up his head,
And you won't be surprised to learn that now Canute is dead.

But if you get up early and walk out on Cleethorpes pier
You'll hear a ghostly whisper if you care to cock an ear:

'I am Canute, an Englishman, this castle is my home!'
His voice will echo wildly in the seething, swirling foam.

But castles built of sand are not as strong as bricks and mortar
And certainly in Cleethorpes, end up ten feet underwater.

*The historical credibility of this work has been questioned by professors of history present at some
poetry readings. The author accepts that the Royal Palace was not in Oldham, but it provided a
supremely elegant rhyme in the first two lines. It is obviously accurate in all other respects.*

DON'T BE SO HEARTLESS

There's a story, which is plausible and I hope not apocryphal, that Tommy Cooper once had a ten minute spot in a variety show. He did his usual trick of putting his head round the curtain and looking like a rabbit in the headlights while he gazed round the theatre and gave a nervous chuckle. This time, instead of regaling the audience with doomed magic tricks and jokes that were so bad they were good, he kept laughing for the full ten minutes. Nothing else, he just laughed, and took the whole theatre with him. By the time he walked off stage the audience was beyond convulsed; it was out of control with the giggles and an unscheduled interval was called to give everyone a chance to calm down.

In recent years the children's show has had a few more outings, although not so many schools these days. We decided to enlist multi-instrumentalist fellow Mandolinquent Richard Collins and drummer Simon Price to help out on some theatre visits. Simon is an extremely fine musician who has played with more than a few big names in the jazz world. To be honest, we weren't sure he'd want to be involved in a children's show, but he loved the idea and we were so glad to have him along. We rehearsed a routine where I would tell the children that during the course of the show they'd get to hear little solos from all the instruments we play... but I wasn't sure we'd have time for a drum solo. As the show progressed, Simon would call out occasionally, asking if it was his time for a solo. It never would be, and just before the last song, I would announce as the final feature a banjo tune played by Richard. By this time the children would be baying for the drums, but I would stand my ground. A few seconds into Richard's solo, Simon would stand from behind his kit, and motion to the audience to keep quiet. He would creep forwards, and to my huge surprise (of course!) would reach over Richard's shoulders and play 'snare drum' on the banjo head as Richard kept going.

All went to plan on our first show together. Throughout the first fifty minutes the children were getting increasingly annoyed with me (the baddie!) as I repeatedly refused drummer Simon's requests for a solo. I finally announced Richard's banjo piece as the 'last' one, Simon pulled his sulkiest face and the children roared their sympathy, but before we could bring the show to its wonderful denouement, a spectacularly well-enunciated seven year old voice, exhibiting all the self-assurance of an Eton-Oxbridge-and-The-Guards educated chairman of the 1922 committee opined to the entire auditorium:
'Oh, for goodness sake! Don't be so heartless!'

A second of silent disbelief was followed by a crescendo of parental and (it has to be said) onstage giggles. A short, unscheduled but necessary interval ensued before Richard played the banjo, Simon played the banjo head, and we sang our final rousing chorus.

The Grand Old Duke Of Pork

Oh, the Grand Old Duke of Pork
He had ten thousand pigs;
He marched them up to the top of the hill
And they all danced Irish jigs.

They danced the longest dance
They'd ever undertaken,
And then they stretched out in the sun
And all turned into bacon.

GREAT EXPECT- ATIONS

Sometimes, the expectations of an audience, maybe through no fault of its own, are quite different from what you're about to offer, or indeed are able to supply. This can often arise when you accept last minute gigs standing in for another artist who has had to cancel.

We were booked at The Stephen Leacock Humour Festival in Orillia, Canada to do a matinee children's show. A Canadian friend had suggested it and sold the idea to the organisers, but it was an oddity of a gig both for us and them. The Leacock Festival's other events were all evening talks by prominent humorous writers, and our own tour was otherwise made up of music festivals and concerts for adults. However, having played extensively to children, we were very happy to accept the date.

Three people and a stray dog turned up in a marquee with four hundred seats and we were understandably disappointed, but of course we did the show. Since we were free that same evening, we bought tickets for another festival event in the same marquee where a Canadian author would be giving a talk and reading from his latest book. That evening the place was packed to the seams but the guest had obviously forgotten all about it and was down the pub in Toronto. A few local stand-up comedians filled in for half an hour and, still hoping he'd appear, an interval was announced. But he didn't appear, and, as all seemed lost and the organisers were preparing to refund everyone's money, we said we could fetch our instruments and do the second half. They jumped at the offer.

So, as we huddle round the solitary microphone, I announce as the first number one of our party pieces, a mandolin and guitar arrangement of Handel's Arrival Of The Queen Of Sheba. This invokes loud guffaws from all four hundred people.

'No, I'm not trying to be funny', I tell them, 'that's what we're going to do.'

Louder guffaws.

'No, really, I should explain, we're not a comedy act.' Unbridled chortling. Man on front row elbows his neighbour ('these Brits are so hilarious!') and I realise what's happening. They're at a humour festival, so they expect it to be humorous. They're laughing even when I've not actually said anything funny; the psychology is extraordinary. So now I milk it and feign offence.

'Please!' - wiping brow in mock exasperation - 'we are musicians of international repute about to play a serious piece of classical music.'

Lady on front row splits her sides and has to be rushed to hospital for stitches while another rolls onto the grass and gives birth to sextuplets. OK, I'm exaggerating, but you get the picture. When we actually performed the piece the crowd went berserk, not in any way because we'd played it better than we normally do, but simply because they'd assumed the mandolin and guitar were props for a comedy act and what they heard was so unexpected. We ended up playing for about 40 minutes and enjoyed one of the best receptions ever... all the time having bought tickets for the privilege!

Old Arthur Blenkinsop had his routine:
Breakfast at 8.00, then at 10.17
Put the kettle on,
And thereupon
Counted the grains of his Nescafé
To make sure they numbered the same today
As they always had,
`Twas his little fad.

His days in the army had taught him precision
In all things, especially the use of his time,
And though all of his peers viewed his ways with derision,
He knew it would help when his life turned to crime.

Old Arthur Blenkinsop had his routine:
Luncheon at 12.00, then at 13.15
Took an omnibus,
And with no fuss
Alighted before the town centre
To check for no impedimenta,
Then did his round
Of his battleground.

He balanced the decadent overproduction
Of all the big shops, but never with greed;
No, his was a trail of more subtle destruction
By taking just those things of which he had need.

LENKINSOP

Diary 1944

Old Arthur Blenkinsop had his routine:
Caught his bus home at 15.13
With his bag of swag,
The old scallywag!
He cooked his potatoes and Grimsby-fresh fish
Or whatever he had for his daily dish;
He worked every day,
It was fresh that way.

As a rogue he adopted no hero, no rival.
No Turpin, no Robin Hood figure was he.
His concern was quite simply his personal survival,
And he cooked up the evidence daily for tea.

Old Arthur Blenkinsop's rigid routine:
Was broken one night. It was 20.13
By the kitchen clock,
When he heard the knock.
The constable gave an apology,
But then with verbose terminology
Took him down the shop -
`Twas an honest cop!

Now aged, with no other means to support him,
Routine is laid down as a guest of the state.
And instinct and military training have taught him
To rejoice where the food appears free on his plate.

Yorkshireman Gardener

A Yorkshireman gardener from Leeds
Was offered some money tree seeds,
But the price tag was such
That he blurted 'Ow much?!
I think I'll mek do wi' me weeds.'

Duck-billed-platypussy

An eccentric old scientist called Hussey,
In his lab was distinctly unfussy.
He crossbred a goose
With an otter and moose;
The result was duck-billed-platypussy.

Collector of Cars

A collector of cars called Ed
Could not pronounce 'R's, so instead
Said 'I love Fewwawis,
But my favouwite caw is
My Wange Wover wespwayed in wed!'

Bashful Nudist

Some friends of a nudist called John
Said 'Come to a party', whereon
He replied 'I'm delighted
To be so invited,
But that day I've got something on.'

Painful Nudist

A newcomer nudist called Pip,
Whose trousers had given him jip,
Said 'What a relief
To be free of the grief
Of my thing getting caught in my zip.'

Composer of Comical Verse

A composer of comical verse
Wrote limericks that somehow were flawed.
He rarely could rhyme
Line three and line four,
And never the first, last and second.

HE'S FROM NORTH OF THE THAMES, DEAR

The mandolin has always had a volume problem, which explains why there are few large scale works written for it. It has no hope of projecting over an orchestra with the same power as a Stradivari violin, a brass instrument, or a Steinway piano, and the comparatively few successful orchestral works that have been written for it display commendable understanding of these qualities by the composer. So the bulk of the mandolin's historic repertoire is in a chamber setting. While the design continues to evolve, even high quality, modern mandolins are still quiet when compared to most other instruments. The invention of the microphone solves the problem of course, and although I still prefer to play completely unamplified, I will always use some subtle sound reinforcement when playing larger venues or those with poor acoustics. I smile politely when I'm told by earnest aficionados that 'good musicians don't need microphones'.

My quartet, The Mandolinquents had been booked to play in a very large church for a classical music festival in the South of England. It was a given that we would need amplification. For reasons best known to itself, the festival had hired in a huge sound system that was of truly rock 'n' roll proportions. There was far too much equipment for our modest needs; towering loudspeakers were aimed down the aisles and the sound mixing desk was bigger than a sofa. Our hearts sank as we arrived, not only because of its visual intrusiveness, but because such testosterone-laden systems are invariably accompanied by engineers with attitude. They usually wear tour jackets emblazoned with the dates of Grunge & the Rock Crunchers' sojourn round Germany in 1989, are fond of reeling off lists of rock royalty they've worked with over the years, and introduce themselves as 'Dave but people usually

all me Gorilla'. Lest anyone
forget, this will be still
legible on a faded forehead
tattoo, and further confirmed
by bleeding knuckles as
their hands trail across
the ground. They have been
involved in so much loud rock
music that they have lost
all the high frequencies
from their own hearing, and,
because they would never
think to get their ears
checked, turn up the treble
frequencies to make it sound
normal' to them. Do that to a
mandolin quartet and we sound
like a hail of ball bearings
bouncing off a skip. We know.
We've been there.

On this occasion, to our
huge relief, the engineer
was no such person, and
was very sensitive to our
requirements. At the sound
check, and indeed at the
concert later on, he balanced
us well and kept the volume
at 'acoustic' rather than
'rock' levels. I was hanging
about the back of the church
before things started, still
in jeans and T-shirt rather
than glad rags, and overheard
two Fortnum-&-Masony, elderly
ladies looking at the sound
mixing desk.
'Oh dear! Look at all this
equipment. I hope they're not
going to be too loud.'
Her vowels were those of a
BBC continuity announcer
from the early days of
broadcasting. I thought I'd
reassure her: 'Excuse me, I
couldn't help but overhear
you. The volume won't be loud,
it'll just be a gentle lift.'
'Well I'm jolly glad to
hear it, young man' (I was
flattered) 'will you be
operating this machine?'
'No. Actually, I'm one of the
musicians.'
'Oooooo!' (Mild swoon,
flutter of eyelashes).
At which point, her friend
chimed in: 'Oh Maud, I'm
getting on a bit now, and I've
always thought it might be
quite a nice way to go to be
blasted out!'
I'm pleased to report that
the old rocker and her friend
were still alive at the end of
the concert.

I chatted to the pair for
a few minutes more, all
the time watched by one of
their husbands. He rocked
gently back and forth with
his hands behind his back,
a furrowed brow and a look
of dreamy incomprehension.
Occasionally he would bark
out 'WHAT?' and I would
repeat something, but he
never actively joined the
conversation. I assumed he
was a little deaf, but after
the seventh or eighth such
interruption his wife turned
to him and explained all.
'He's from north of the Thames
dear.'

PIGEON PI

Some pigeons lived in the old yew tree,
So dense, so bushy, so tall.
Each morning they'd swoop in a loop to the roof,
Then fall to the garden wall.

'Pigeons! Pigeons!' the young lad cried
As he eyed his avian guests.
'How many? How many?' the cook replied,
'This morning have left their nests?'

He carefully counted the corpulent birds
Then pronounced his precocious reply:
'3.142 and a bit –
Enough for a pigeon pi.'

GAMBLER

The psychiatrist told me, 'Stop gambling.
You'll lose all your cash if you don't.'
He said he was sure he could cure me.
I answered 'I'll wager you won't.'

ROGUE AND ROSE

If once you thought a rose by any other name
Would smell so sweet
Well thinker, think again!
For no grand Latin tag could so convey this lipsticked thorn
Upon whose stalk, neath painted petals, vengeful barbs are born,
On guard to lacerate
The flesh of those
Who roses
Cultivate.

If once you thought a rogue by any other name
Would thieve and cheat,
Well thinker, think again!
What 'common thief' would grace his face with laughing, twinkling eyes?
Or kindly gaze on those in need, his trade to compromise?
Or share with ease his beer
With those whom he
May soon force flee
In fear?

If once you thought a bee by any other name
Would fly so fleet,
Well thinker, think again!
What finer word could well reflect the intellect, the skill
Of one who, motionless in flight, would take the dust at will
From flowers, and yet still knows
To blithely scorn
The lurking thorn
Upon that rogue, the rose.

ДОРЕВОЛЮЦИОННЫЙ

As years pass, memories of school days inevitably fade. Those that remain are, I suppose, of things that meant a lot at the time. The day the school bogs exploded was a case in point. It meant a huge amount to me. It really left a burning impression. Not that I had anything to do with it, you understand. It was an anonymous hero who brought our dreaded headmaster to the school hall for assembly the next morning. He stormed from one side of the stage to the other, his black gown sweeping behind at an unfeasibly near-horizontal angle, face bloated in purple rage, cane a-swishing, demanding to know who was responsible. As our stomachs knotted with suppressed giggles, he was frustrated by our collective silence. To the mysterious culprit I offer my profound gratitude.

For rather gentler reasons, memories of Russian lessons remain equally vivid. Our teacher was a man who to generations of pupils had been known as Boris, and so he shall be called here. No, it wasn't his real name, but neither was it a cruel nickname. Some teachers deserved a cutting satire, but Boris was genial and immensely likeable. His nickname echoed his subject and was deservedly affectionate.

There were strong rumours, again passed down the generations, that he had been a bit of a hero during World War Two, his linguistic skills playing a part. Occasionally, we would get to hear a little 'war wound' at the end of a lesson, but in general terms rather than in any detail. It was enough to whet our appetites for the language and the culture of a very foreign country. Sadly, Boris died shortly after I left school.

Despite a very different career path, I had always retained a love for the Russian language. You don't even have to understand it; the sound alone has a

АРИСТОКРАТ

eculiar beauty and its
ntonation is tinged with
beguiling melancholy. It
as always easy for those
earning French or German
o keep in practice, but
ntil the fall of the Eastern
loc, meeting a Russian for
ome conversation was nigh
mpossible. So my abilities
lipped over the years;
peaking a language, I soon
iscovered, was not like
iding a bike.

ne day, The Mandolinquents
ere invited to play at a
rivate party. It's not the
ort of invitation we'd
sually accept, but this
ounded interesting. A
roup of largely retired
rofessional (or very good
amateur) string players were
meeting in a remote corner
of Wales for a residential
week where they would do
little else but eat, sleep
and play string quartets.
Many were former members
of the BBC Philharmonic
and Halle orchestras. One
evening they would hire in
some entertainment, and on
this occasion it was us. No
pressure! They turned out to
be a most generous audience,
and we ate with them and
stayed the night afterwards.

About half way through the
meal we discovered that the
wife of one of the organisers
was Russian and I was cheered
into attempting to engage
in Slavic dialogue. Shy and
reticent at first, I soon
became fuelled by the fluency
that only a couple of bottles
of beer can bring, and
surprised myself at how much
I remembered. Wide-eyed in
astonishment, my partner in
conversation kept me sweating
for a couple of minutes before
switching to heavily accented
English.
'It amazing to hear you speak
so well, but nobody in Russia
use accent like that anymore.
You have accent of pre-
revolutionary aristocrat.'

Thank you, Boris!

65

Gerunding

A professor of English called Rawling
Was explaining a gerund, but stalling,
Then recalled with elation
His stated vocation
Was: 'Gerunding serves as my calling'.

Grammar

If grammar were merely adjunctive,
And failed to make prose more conjunctive,
We'd get in a mess
With apostrophe stress
And all think subjunctive's defunctive.

Syllable surplus

A wordsmith who hailed from the Humber
Said 'What's guaranteed to encumber
My poetic purpose
Is syllable surplus
Enforcing my use of enjambe -
... ment.'

Verbs

A student of English called Spence
Of verbs could make limited sense.
He read each paradigm,
But the concept of time
Was a subject that made him feel... tense.

Verbing

A pattern of speech that needs curbing
Is one both perverse and perturbing:
The American trend,
Guaranteed to offend,
Of garbaging language by verbing.

Word Perfect

If your literary style needs a boost,
Then by no foreign brogue be seduced,
For it never takes long
In our own English tongue
To adeptly deploy *le mot juste*.

Malapropisms

And lastly, allow me to mention
A sauce of some linguistic tension,
That malapropisms
Create verbal schisms
Pacifically incomprehension.

ACROSS THE POND

All professions have their own folklore, their own mythology, tales of unexpected turns of event and outright cock-ups which may or may not have happened to the storyteller. It's always funnier of course when the profession is one's own. I can't believe there is a single musician who has watched the cult film This Is Spinal Tap and not cried with laughter at the hapless rock band on tour. Although a fiction, it depicts universal musical truths, and is fundamentally one huge 'in' joke, which, to its credit, manages to appeal beyond those of us who are 'in'. Musical references aside, we can all enjoy the deflation of ego, the bubbles of pomposity being well and truly pricked! But through the laughter, the scenes strike an unsettling chord for musicians (say, an Em/maj9) because such things have happened to us all.

Perhaps because of the inherent cultural divide, trips to North America have provided the most fertile breeding ground. On our very first concert, the reaction of the American audience was most shocking. Whooping and hollering from the outset, they rose to their feet in a prolonged cheer after the final note; we almost ducked for cover in case a few firearms were discharged into the ceiling. Maybe we'd watched too many cowboy films, but it all brought an unexpected thrill to two bemused performers. A few days into the tour, it became evident that standing ovations were par for the course Stateside. Deserved or not, who were we to argue with such a show of appreciation? Not terribly British, maybe, but always deeply appreciated. It was equally perplexing to return to England, where culture shock worked in reverse for a while, and those over-the-top receptions were sorely missed.

Of course, an English accent never fails in the USA. Stopping somewhere for a coffee, it became good sport to induce half-embarrassed giggles from baristas by trowelling on the flat Yorkshire vowels to the tipping point of incomprehension. On one gig, I would let the audience know that the main reason we loved touring the States was not the enthusiastic receptions or lavish hospitality we received, but because we loved their accent – it was so cute! On another, after having been introduced as the most charming and delightful people our host had ever met, I promptly declared myself to be in a foul mood. The audiences loved the humour, and very quickly dissuaded me from the profoundly ungenerous myth that irony is the preserve of the Brits.

The sheer size of the USA demands internal flights when touring, and fellow passengers were invariably chatty.
'D'ya want some reading material?' an elderly man smiled.
'That's awfully kind of you, old chap.'
'Sure. Got a whole bunch of magazines here.'
He passed across about a dozen copies of Responsible Hand Gun Owner and a lone copy of USA Today, which Hilary read.
'You're not interested in hand guns?'
'We don't have them in England. It's against the law.'
'No guns! But your police, they must have guns?'
'Not routinely, only specialist officers.'
'So none of your friends carry guns?'
'No, none.'
His incredulity rose. 'But whadd'ya do if a wolf attacks your cows?'
'We don't have cows in England.'

ur naivety surrounding the whole firearms issue never truly resolved. In the days before he whole world was on email, I needed to write ome and was looking for somewhere I might buy riting paper and envelopes. Driving south rom Brattleboro, Vermont, I saw a sign saying eneral Store and, assuming the problem solved, pulled the car over and entered the shop. It ook a few seconds to take in, but all I saw as ammunition. Box after box of ammunition, tacked high on the floor. I looked round the helves and it was the same story. I turned, nd behind the main counter saw a long row of ifles on the wall, and a myriad handguns in he display cabinet. Between the two stood man of about two metres... and easily the ame height. He stared slightly away from me who-knows-what and gave not the slightest ndication of being aware that a customer had ntered the shop.

here are times in one's life when, even before e words have left the lips, pangs of regret te deep, and this was one.
xcuse me, old chap, do you have any writing aper?'
e slowly shuffled a half turn to face me, but is eyes remained focused beyond my head. here was a disturbing pause before he replied a menacingly slow drawl.
robably not.'

Even after several trips across the Atlantic it was still a mistake to think the place was becoming truly familiar. We had to return a rented car to Grand Rapids Airport, Michigan, before catching a flight to some other god-forsaken Midwestern town. It was in the days before satellite navigation and I was lost, although I knew I was somewhere near the airport. A handy petrol station appeared. I stopped for the obligatory refuel before returning the car, and while paying asked the man in the kiosk if he knew the way to the airport.
'Airport? Which airport?'
'Well, err... Grand Rapids Airport.'
'You mean the one up on 44th?'
'I don't know... yes, probably.'
'... ain't no other airport.'
I smiled nervously and waited. After what seemed like an eternity he remembered my original question and, taking a deep breath, gave me directions. I thanked him and was about to leave.
'Say, whereabouts you from?'
'England.'
'England, huh? I figured you's from somewhere.'

SHE TALKS TO ME SOMETIMES

She talks to me sometimes at four in the morn,
Soft moans and low whispers in slumbering flight.
Her eyes, like butterfly wings on chaotic course
That, if I will hard, just might
Fly her back to me at dawn.

I tenderly rest on her brow with my fingertips,
Calming her turbulence, settling her squalls.
My touch moves to steady her unsettled eyes
And, as would a beacon of morning light, calls
Her down to land on cotton slips.

THE KISSING GATE

In summer they walked, trudging the hills and lanes,
Gathering berries and crabs with no chance to be eaten,
Talking just talk, daydreaming, pondering,
Singing their made-up songs and wandering
Fields so warm and wheaten.

And after the field, they reached the kissing gate.
They paused at first, and then, with love anew,
Cross cedar bars they sparred like two possessed
And raced on home to give their best
To what the young must do.

And now the crusts of greying snow they tramp.
No matter the weather, no matter the chilly tide.
Come winter, they ramble the old, familiar routes,
Snapping the wheaty stubs in easy boots
In fields where field mice hide.

And after the field, before the path winds on,
The cedar bars, still strong, invite their rest. They wait,
And there, where lips had first sparked fire, still strong,
Still white burns their desire, and long
They linger at the kissing gate.

A ROUNDABOUT FASHION

At the risk of sounding like an inspiration for Monty Python's Four Yorkshiremen sketch, there wasn't much money kicking about when I was young. Further education would have been unthinkable without the grant available at the time, and being strapped for cash remained the status quo well into adulthood. Despite this, the aforementioned sketch to this day has me breaking out into an uncontrollable half-smile whenever I see it, and has provided minutes of mild amusement over the years.

Even before student life had ended, we had adventurously set out on a career in music without agent or manager, but we were acutely aware that the most important missing item was a car. Our problems in this respect were twofold: we couldn't afford one and neither of us could drive.

Playing what could loosely be described as 'folk', we decided to embark on the well worn path of paying our dues by doing unpaid spots at folk clubs as warm-ups to the main guest in the hope of receiving a proper, paid booking at some future date. We used what bus services were available and begged lifts from friends to visit all the clubs within striking distance of home. It soon became apparent that we needed to travel further afield in our mission, and hitching was to be the solution. It turned out to be remarkably easy. Provided there was space in the vehicle, a couple carrying a guitar, violin, mandolin and double bass(!) offered an enticing challenge to drivers. Sometimes we would stay overnight with people we knew, but, emboldened by our successful thumbs, we would often hitch back to Reading late at night. All went well on a few such trips, until the day we visited a club in Brighton. I really cannot recall how well our spot went, or whether it resulted in a proper booking, but we decided to hitch home that same night. We made it as far as Ascot, by which time it was about 1.30am. There were only a few cars passing, but someone took us to Bracknell

were now just ten miles
om home.

, like me, you love
oundabouts, you'll find
acknell fascinating, even
ore so, I would suggest,
an Milton Keynes. In
K, with its soulless grid
ttern, roundabouts
ickly become predictable,
variably of similar size
d with just four roads
iting at neat, 90 degree
gles. Frankly, if you've
en one MK roundabout,
u've seen them all. In
acknell, devoid of any
id system, roundabouts are
oyous, springing on you when
u least expect them, and
fering a dazzling variety
sizes, shapes, coverings
d numbers of exits. Some are
rcular, some elliptical;
ere are doubles too: double
nis, and larger ones,
ich, when seen from above,
e as beautiful as images
colliding stars taken
from the Hubble telescope.
Some are in such close
proximity that the resulting
one-way system assumes an
asymmetrical figure of
eight with all the grace of
an art nouveau line. And
how I love their names: Twin
Bridges, Coral Reef, Running
Horse, Mill Pond. The one
regret about Bracknell is
that there is no satellite
roundabout, and for that
pressing reason its residents
are acutely jealous of Hemel
Hempstead, High Wycombe and
of course the jewel in the
roundabout crown, Swindon.
But my enthusiasm may become
infectious.

It was by one such roundabout
at about 2.30am that our luck
ran out. With just one car
having passed in the last
forty minutes, the place was
eerily quiet and all we could
hear emanating from the
surrounding office blocks
was the whirr of computers of
the then embryonic hi-tech
industry. We knew we would
not be seeing our bed that
night, but, resourceful to
the end, we were carrying a
little tent. Until now, we
hadn't been stranded, but
had always assumed that if
we were, it would be out in
the country and a farmer's
field would be available for
a quick shut-eye. Here, there
were no fields. And so it came
to pass, that in the middle
of the night we pitched
our tiny orange tent on a
Bracknell roundabout, fell
fast asleep, and were woken
just a few hours later by
the rising roar of commuter
traffic and the sniffles
of an inquisitive Labrador
crossing the road with his
owner. We pushed our heads
out. A police car circled
twice, but left us in peace
and we quickly struck camp
and hitched an easy lift to
Reading.

HOW TO WRITE
A TUNE

I was playing my scales and arpeggios,
Melodic minors – three octaves at that!
They bore me stiff like God alone knows;
Just when am I likely to play in D-flat?

But then, without warning, I made a mistake,
And then came another: a second, a third.
They tickled my ears so I played a re-take,
This time with determined intent they be heard.

I jiggled my notes, adding doodles and diddles.
I toyed with the rhythm. Slips needn't sound rotten!
I gilded them blithely with twists, turns and twiddles,
My scales and arpeggios now long forgotten.

So if writer's block looms its head (just supposing)
While fervently forging your fugue and toccata,
Then remember this tale, and know that composing
Is oft about making the most of errata.

MARRY ME, MELODY

'Marry me, Melody!' the pompous Lyrics cried,
'For you can't tell your story all alone.'
'Indeed I can', the Melody replied,
'And best for each that story be their own'.

PERFECT
FIFTH

It's 3am and here – awake – I lie,
And follow soft, white shapes in inky black,
Entranced, as milky moonbeams through my window fly
And bounce from silvered glass, a vain but moving lullaby
For this bemused insomniac.

So should I rise or longer lie awake?
If, gently, through the bedroom door I creep
And then downstairs, some soothing camomile I'll take.
But no! Two hinges sing, one high, one low, and join to make
A perfect fifth. But still she sleeps.

It's 4am and I must back to bed;
Once more the charms of deepest slumber beckon.
And there, still peacefully my loved one rests her head.
And as I lie, her nostrils sing the interval I dread:
A wretched, rasping minor second.

THE COUNTERTENOR AND THE CRITIC

esuited, slim, with poise he takes the stage,
nd, motionless, attends the violins,
ne wind, until The Barbican he wins
ith full soprano. JC Bach has come of age.

critic's pride? Well (modesty aside!)
s wit is wild as Dottie Parker's quill.
e'll weaponise his nimble words until
e's slayed the lot! But ssh! Tonight he'll hide

home. This time the wrap is plain to see.
et up. Cork popped. For one and sorry all
e'll blindly scrawl his sad, sepulchral gall:
'e have JS, so why embrace JC?'

eanwhile, three curtain calls befall, and we
ith glee await part two expectantly.

*e French countertenor Philippe Jaroussky performed a programme of JC Bach and Handel at The Barbican, London, to an ecstatic reception, including
ee long curtain calls even before the interval. One disparaging press notice the following day referred to the 'lukewarm response', bringing into
estion that critic's very presence at the concert.*

FIREFLIES

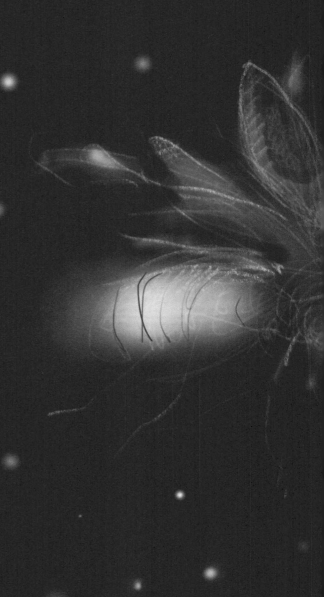

Still, the lake at evening,
Where fireflies neath dark skies
Dance and glow on watery blue,
And vie with stars to cast a hue,
As fireflies do.

Still, the lake at evening,
Where fish sleep in pools deep.
Fallen wind and fallen sun
Let water boatmen journey on,
As boatmen do.

Still, the lake at evening,
With my hand in your hand,
Sharing stillness with the lake,
But soon the twilight peace will break,
As dancing, glowing, love awakes,
As fireflies do.

WHY, OH WHY IS HAY-ON-WYE?

The faux-foxed ladies of Hay-on-Wye
Delicately slurp bespoke pumpkin soup from jumble sale spoons.
And pay the price!
How rustic! How *de nos jours!*
'Akin, you know, to *potage aux legumes*
Eddie and I had in Roscoff when we
Motored to Lausanne this Spring.'

Little Miranda, free-range parent,
Knows the world revolves around her son,
Who, in an orgy of free expression,
Wobbles our foamless cappuccinos
By his undisciplined table-top dance.

Dusty bookshops, fusty tombs
Of long-dead tomes,
The bulk of which would stand no chance
To grace our homes.
So do I laugh? Or do I cry...
'Why, oh why is Hay-on-Wye?'

SHEFFIELD STEEL WORKS 1959

With gloves of heavy leather, aprons too,
And steel-cupped toes, they'd sweat a grim day through.
And men would die, like me, like you.

No banter passed above the white-noised roar.
One lonely Anglo-Saxon tone might soar,
As did a century before.

So, swing the furnace doors! Let's see the gates
Of hell, and how the brooding lava waits.
A heat, past white, intimidates.

Now flowing, slowing, channelled, cooling fast.
Twisted, turned by giant tongues, harassed
By hardened men. Tamed, at last.

Put on your softest kid gloves when we meet.
No channelling, no twisting tongues. My heat
Is but the white of meadowsweet.

ldhood visits to the Sheffield steel works of J Beardshaw & Sons, my father's place of work, left a burning impression.

OTHER PEOPLES' CUSTOMS

We had always been aware that Canada had a markedly different vibe from that of its chrome-plated neighbour the USA, but there were similarities, too. Landing at Toronto with some CDs, we declared them to the immigration officer.

'You'll need to pay import duty on these. Go to that window over there

The most bizarre conversation ensued.

'What's your reason for entering Canada?'

'We're musicians. We're playing at Goderich Celtic Festival'

'Yeah? I was there in 2012. A buddy of mine talked me into going.'

'Oh really? We were there in 2012 as well.'

'Y'know what? I HATE CELTIC MUSIC!'

'errr........!'

'Y'know what else? I had a great time in spite of that 'cause the atmosphere was so good. No charge. Have a nice day!'

American customs could be equally entertaining.

'What exactly are these CDs for?' the man asked Hilary

'Some for sale, some promotional'

'I'm gonna have to charge you tax on these... let me have a look.' He rummaged in the case and pulled out a copy of Hilary's first album.

'Hey, dat's you on the cover!'

'It's me'

'You're Hilary James, huh? Hey, you're famous, just look at dat....' he turned to me: 'So who are you?'

I had a feel for the situation now and pulled out one of my albums.

'That's me' I said, removing my spectacles to match the cover photo.

'So you're famous too?'

(If in doubt, lie) 'Yup.'

'Hey, Chuck, come and look at dis... I got two stars here. You know what These CDs are no big deal, move along please.'

The status of a z-list celebrity is all that mandolin players can realistically hope to achieve, particularly in the UK where the instrument occupies an even smaller musical backwater than in some other countries. But why would anyone hope for more? The benefits of being able to make a living out of music while still being able to walk down the street without being pestered by fans and paparazzi are enormous. Nevertheless, having lived in the same town for over forty years, having played countless local concerts and held a long residency at a local arts centre with my quartet The Mandolinquents, I do occasionally get recognised when I'm out and about.

Often this is by people who say hello and expect me to remember they were in the tenth row, third seat along last February... you get the picture. My memory for faces is at best terrible, and I have tried hard to cope with it over the years. I will always smile and return a greeting but my glazed stare probably betrays my lack of recognition.

Such an occasion happened outside my own house one day as I was chatting with a neighbour. A man walking up the street was smiling at me and waved; I didn't recognise him but went into damage limitation mode and gave a half-wave back, a move famously perfected by our own monarch as she surveys the crowds from the balcony of Buck House.
'Hello!' he beamed as he got a little closer.
'Hello!' I returned, hiding bewilderment.
He got right up to me: 'Oh, it's not you.'
'It is me, actually.'
'No, it's someone who looks like you.'
'I assure you, it absolutely is me.'
'No, no, you just do a good impersonation.'
He trudged off up the road.

I HAVE BEEN EXPECTING YOU

By half way through the second year of my degree in Russian I had become so disenchanted with the course, and positively enchanted with the prospect of a career in music, that I announced to my tutor that I would drop out. He successfully spent an entire morning talking me out of the idea. It never struck me until years later, that if I had departed, the drop out rate for my year would have been 100 percent - I was his only student! But in those days, it wasn't just about the academic qualification and job prospects. It was about the whole university experience, broadening the mind, staying up all night talking about the meaning of life and so on. Best of all, I had my year abroad to look forward to.

With just a few exceptions, it wasn't possible to get British students into Russian universities in the 1970s, but a Polish one beckoned, and the prospect of a year behind the Iron Curtain was enticing. And so I set off for Poznan in 1974. I was excited to get my first view of the East, and as the train juddered to a halt at Friedrichstrasse station, right on the Berlin Wall, I put my head out of the window. I looked west for a moment, then turned to look east to be greeted by a gun barrel quivering an inch from my nose and its owner barking something in German. I didn't need to understand, and beat a hasty retreat. Later that day I unpacked my suitcase in a sparsely furnished room of a drab student high rise block known as Akumulatory (batteries) because of the large sign on its roof. Both block and sign still stand, a testament to the durability of communist construction.

I quickly realised that I wasn't going to learn much Russian. Poles were forced to learn the language of their Soviet masters, but would never speak it willingly. Still today, my closest encounter with death remains the occasion just a few days into my Poznan experience when I bought a Russian newspaper and sat in a cafe eading it. Suffice to say the big geezers at the next table ere not impressed.

 couple of days later, still n my first week, there was an nexpected knock at my door. man smiled, resplendent n an expensive pinstriped uit, brolly over arm, bowler at in one hand and – here's he crunch – a copy of that orning's Times in the other. Mr Mayor? How do you do? he name's Kobylanski.' He poke in perfectly enunciated eceived pronunciation. re you English?' I asked, little confused by this tereotypical city gent with Polish name.
ood Lord, no! I'm Polish, ld boy. I have a little usiness proposition for you; ay I come in?' was intrigued; he sat down n the one easy chair in y room and placed his hat nd newspaper on the table. he cryptic crossword was

completed, and there was little doubt he'd wanted me to notice the fact. Mr Kobylanski, it turned out, ran evening classes in English conversation and he asked if I, with my obvious qualifications as a native speaker, would be willing to lead some. We chatted for a few minutes. It was only because he had told me he was Polish that I could detect any accent, but I had to listen very, very hard. He spoke with a fluency and a command of idiomatic English I have rarely heard in a foreigner. Perhaps the one giveaway was that he had obviously absorbed some ancient book of English proverbs and sayings, and was fond of peppering his speech with archaisms. Eventually he dropped this bombshell: 'I notice you have a South Yorkshire accent; are you able to speak RP?' A Pole had detected my

Sheffield accent!! I could indeed speak received pronunciation, I told him, but couldn't guarantee I could keep it up for the length of a conversation class. He said he didn't want his students speaking with a regional accent, so, if I wouldn't mind?

I think I lasted three weeks. I was then sacked by a foreigner for not speaking my own language well enough. Not many people can make that claim.

It wasn't as if I needed the extra money. The grant I received was generous. I often ate in restaurants, bought books and lots of sheet music, and generally had a good time. But by Christmas I was homesick and decided to head back to England until early January, even though the original plan had been to stay out for the whole academic year.

Mid December found me sitting on a sluggish train trundling across West Germany and panicking. I had received bad advice from some other students in Akumulatory, who had told me it was cheaper to buy separate tickets to cross the countries of northern Europe rather than just one from Poznan to Calais. As I looked at my cash I knew there was not enough. I had no credit card, nothing. An elderly man boarded the train and sat opposite me in the same compartment, saying something by way of a greeting. I apologised for not being able to speak German but it was no problem as he spoke excellent English. Our conversation flowed easily for the next hour; I learned about his successful business, he about my student life in Reading and Poznan. I never mentioned a word about my plight, but a very strange thing happened. He announced it was his station and, thanking me profusely for the chat, offered a handshake as he left. He then pressed a bundle of notes into my palm and with his other hand closed my fingers round them, muttering quiet apologies about what had happened during the war. He turned swiftly and made no further eye contact, and I looked down at my ticket home.

Hilary joined me for the last six weeks of my stay and we travelled south to the mountain resort of Zakopane for a holiday. A Polish friend had arranged a week's break for us on a farm about a mile outside the town. A new house had been built specifically for B&B, while the family (Mum, Dad, children, Grandma and cows) shared an old shed across the yard. Any linguistic communication was out of the question, but it didn't matter. The farmer showed us the al fresco toilets sporting an interesting thirty foot drop the old newspaper torn into, err..., handy sized pieces, and presented us with a huge rye loaf and a dozen eggs. Breakfast for the week, we thought.

The next evening we were convinced our time had come. He burst into the room, and with a vodka induced wobble brandished a huge knife. He beckoned us to follow him down to the cellar and we thought it best to obey. Hanging from the ceiling by its trotters was a whole pig. He raised the knife and, despite his inebriation, managed to cut a long slither of fat, nearly the whole length of the animal. He tipped his head back, slid it down his throat, then with a golden-toothed grin handed u the weapon and magnanimousl offered his pig.

e didn't want to repeat the experience and chose to leave arly and get back late each ay. On our last morning e had two eggs left, just nough for breakfast before e returned to Poznan. Our ost arrived, sober this time nd brandishing another ozen, his trademark grin n place. We tried as best we ould to explain we didn't eed them, but he decided he as going to cook for us. It as a simple meal, a twelve gg omelette fried in 500 rams of butter. We ate, olite to the last, and with ur stomachs heavy in our oots, headed for the train.

ot long after that we left oland, or at least Hilary id. At the East German order the Polish guards oarded the train asking or passports. Hilary's was ecked and returned, mine as pocketed by the guard, o said something I couldn't understand. He marched off and came back a minute later with his friend; they took control of an armpit each and lifted me off the train. Hilary and I had ten pounds between us and we managed to take five each before we were separated. The train left and I was locked in a border post with no clue what was going on, visions of extended Siberian holidays looming. They eventually found someone who spoke enough English to explain to me that, because of my extended visa, I needed a document from the police confirming that I was not wanted for any criminal offence before I would be allowed to leave. This was big news to me, but I had no choice. They put me on a train back to Poznan and told me to go down to the police station the next morning. What followed was like something straight out of James Bond. After an interminable wait, which I suspect was more for their amusement than necessity, I was shown into a room where a senior officer rocked back, testing the strength of his chair's rear legs. He eyed me over his feet which were up on the edge of his desk:

'Ah! Meesterrr Mayorrr! Ah heff bin expectink you.'

With no fuss, I was handed the necessary document and left Poland the next day.

Soft piles of rotting, russet leaves conspired to hide
The Stick. And, cradled in its gutter-bed beside
The lane, alone,
Unheeded, thrown,
It rocked at times in slipstreams blown
From passing tractor wheels. As winter gripped,
It chilled beneath the snows the wind had whipped.

By Pateley Bridge one grey November day I'd cast
It down. But patiently it lay until, at last,
The springtime rain
And waters, draining
Hard from melting fells, again
Would wash it, fresh, awake, and it might hail
The first who'd walk in wakening Nidderdale.

I *was* the first that spring. In dubbined boots I strode
The lane, and eyed the stick that thawed and glowed
In watery sun.
I passed, then spun,
And asked aloud, in joyful fun:
'Are you *The Stick*? Tell me, if you can talk'.
Then swore I heard The Stick reply: 'Let's walk.'

'You'll be my staff once more?' I asked, 'my trusted guide?'
'I'll teach you how this valley breathes', The Stick replied,
'For I can show
The path I know
Of old. To Middlesmoor we'll go.'
We walked, and found a pace, now slow, now fast,
That matched the clouds, some high, some low that passed.

We drank the air; we drank the Nidd, newborn and clean.
We climbed the field where hungry Mr Fox had been,
Until, ahead,
The watershed
Appeared. The Stick then said:
'Just lay me gently; rest me by the lane.
Someone will walk to Pateley Bridge again.'

Hilary James

With an ambition to spend half a life in music and half in art, singer, mando-bassist, guitarist, artist and illustrator Hilary James is now very close to achieving that state of euphoria.

After a degree in fine art at Reading University she spent many years singing for her supper, recording five acclaimed solo albums and partnering Simon Mayor both as a duo and with his mandolin quartet The Mandolinquents.

Her brushes, crayons and, more recently, a worrying addiction to her tablet computer and digital pencil were all deployed in illustrating this book.

hilaryjames.com